YOUR
ORIGINS
MATTER

Henry M. Morris III

INSTITUTE FOR
CREATION
RESEARCH

Dallas, Texas
www.icr.org

Dr. Henry M. Morris III holds four earned degrees, including a D.Min. from Luther Rice Seminary and the Presidents and Key Executives MBA from Pepperdine University. A former college professor, administrator, business executive, and senior pastor, Dr. Morris is an articulate and passionate speaker frequently invited to address church congregations, college assemblies, and national conferences. The eldest son of ICR's founder, Dr. Morris has served for many years in conference and writing ministry. His love for the Word of God and passion for Christian maturity, coupled with God's gift of teaching, have given Dr. Morris a broad and effective ministry over the years. He has authored numerous articles and books, including *The Big Three: Major Events that Changed History Forever; Exploring the Evidence for Creation; 5 Reasons to Believe in Recent Creation; The Book of Beginnings, Vol. 1: Creation, Fall, and the First Age; The Book of Beginnings, Vol. 2: Noah, the Flood, and the New World; Pulling Down Strongholds: Achieving Spiritual Victory through Strategic Offense; A Firm Foundation: Devotional Insights to Help You Know, Believe, and Defend Truth;* and *Six Days of Creation.*

YOUR ORIGINS MATTER
by Henry M. Morris III, D.Min.

First printing: October 2013

All Scripture quotations are from the New King James Version.

ISBN: 978-1-935587-37-8

Please visit our website for other books and resources: www.icr.org

Printed in the United States of America.

Table of Contents

∾ 1 ∾
You Are Not an Accident

Somewhere in our search for identity, all of us eventually ask, "What am I?" That question goes to the core of how we see ourselves and how we function. Usually, we ask other questions first, like "How did I get here?" or "Where do babies come from?" Most answers we get in those early years are pretty vague. The stork or Santa Claus or the hospital works for a while, but we find that most folks avoid really answering the question—other than *finally* giving us "the talk" about our biological beginning.

Religious Answers

Religious institutions score a bit better. Usually, catechism structures open with a question like "Who made me?" The common answer is "God made me." Although generally correct, the thought is still somewhat vague. How, one wonders, does God make me?

Most religions don't deal with the fundamental question very much at all. More attention is given to what God expects us to do and how we are to treat others—all of which is important, but *what* I am makes a huge difference in my understanding of how to live, who or what to worship, and how to relate to the rest of life on the planet.

Most of the Western world is monotheistic—i.e., believing in one "God" who is ultimately responsible for the existence of the universe and to whom all intelligent life will one day respond. But the variations on this theme are many and diverse. How can we choose what to believe? How can we possibly know what is true? The differences are profound and, of course, impact the framework through which we view the world.

Academic Answers

An enormous amount of our formative years is spent in academic institutions. In the Western world, we enter the formal educational system when we are very young, and many of us continue in school through our young adult years. The teachers employed to teach us are trained in the colleges and universities of our culture. The professors who teach the teachers are themselves products of many years of immersion in the academic world.

It should come as no surprise that the overwhelming majority of the academic community does not encourage the idea that God even exists, much less "makes" us or has anything to do with who or what we are. We spend far more time in school than we do in church, synagogue, or mosque. What do you suppose affects our thinking the most?

Scientific Answers

The main reason that the academic world is overwhelmingly atheistic or pantheistic—or philosophically humanistic and naturalistic—is because the scientific world has embraced the idea that all life has developed "accidentally" over eons of random interaction with chemicals and gases, making you and me nothing more than complex assemblies of molecules with no purpose and no meaning other than to reproduce and survive.

All of us are familiar with the basic premise of Charles Darwin. He insisted that every living thing shares a common ancestor that developed over time through natural selection. Darwin's theory was not really new but synthesized the ideas of 18th-century naturalists who had devised intricate technical theories to explain away an intelligent "First Cause" of the universe.

Although we are now well into the second decade of the 21st century, the science we depend on and the philosophy that drives the science are built on the commitment of the master teachers of the elite universities that dominated secular thinking during the 1990s.

For example, Peter Atkins insisted that we are "just a bit of slime on a planet."[1] How's that for a great perspective? Stephen Weinberg concluded that humanity is a "more-or-less farcical outcome of a chain of accidents"—a living "joke" in the universe among its endless accidental events.[2] Richard Dawkins, the popular evolutionary spokesman, calls the human genetic code the blind programming of "robot vehicles,"[3] and Sir Fred Hoyle, one of the more famous astronomers and mathematicians of Europe, postulated that living creatures were "no more than ingenious machines that have evolved as strange by-products in an odd corner of the universe."[4]

These older quotes represent the arrogant philosophy that continues to direct every discipline in the academic world. Almost everything we read, see, and hear follows the evolutionary storyline that you and I are nothing more than the result of eons of random accidents in a purposeless and meaningless universe.

If the majority of what we are taught is so secular and atheistic, why then do national polls calculate that large majorities of the educated and intellectual Western world still believe in a personal and transcendent God? Why, when our educational system is dominated by evolutionary naturalism, do those same polls show that nearly half of the population still believes in creation?[5]

Perhaps the Gallup and Pew organizations have made a mistake. After all, church attendance has been declining for decades, and the churches, synagogues, and mosques have been dominated by moral and ethical (and political) teachings to the apparent exclusion of any teaching about a Creator God. Young adults are leaving their religious backgrounds in droves, and a significant minority of the younger population lists "none" as their religious affiliation. Why does the idea of a "real" God persist?

Biblical Answers

Perhaps it is because...

> The heavens declare the glory of God; And the firmament shows His handiwork. Day unto day utters speech, And night unto night reveals knowledge. There is no speech nor language Where their voice is not heard. (Psalm 19:1-3)

Perhaps the obvious "language" of the earth and the creatures that thrive on it are so full of answers that we can

> Ask the beasts, and they will teach you; And the birds of the air, and they will tell you; Or speak to the earth, and it will teach you; And the fish of the sea will explain to you. Who among all these does not know That the hand of the LORD has done this, In whose hand is the life of every living thing, And the breath of all mankind? (Job 12:7-10)

Perhaps the answers are "clearly seen, being understood by the things that are made" (Romans 1:20). Evidently, in spite of the many efforts to persuade us that God either does not exist or is irrelevant, the Creator Himself has made sure that the entire universe "speaks" with a language that can be heard by every person.

The Language of the Universe

Just what is it that the universe says to us? Well, to begin with, it clearly tells us that it could not create itself! Science verifies what is often called the First Law. That is, everything that exists is in a state of conservation. Nothing can be created or destroyed. The various forms of energy can be changed, augmented, and transferred from other sources, but the total amount of that mass-energy remains the same. If anything can be called an absolute fact, this First Law is as sure as anything we can know.

This information is really important! That law tells ("speaks to") us that nothing that exists today could cause itself to come into being. There must have been a beginning. And that beginning would have to involve processes, information, and energies that we have no knowledge of. Scientists argue all the time about what and when the beginning may have happened, but everyone knows that there must have been one.

And the Second Law tells us that every time work is done in the universe—every time anything happens—the energy necessary to make the event happen becomes "used." Some portion of the constant *quantity* of energy in the universe (the First Law) becomes unavailable for further work. The energy turns inward—the *quality* deteriorates. That measureable deterioration is called entropy and it *always* increases over time, causing everything in the universe to "die"—slowly, but surely. Again, if there is anything that can be called a law of the universe, this Second Law is demonstrated in everything all the time. Everything wears out. Everything goes toward a state of disorder and ultimately becomes unusable. Everything! No exceptions.

Oh, we can delay the inevitable by taking energy or order or information from something or somewhere else—but all that we are doing is transferring or changing or augmenting. There is no creation going on. And since all activity over time goes toward a condition of unavailable and non-usable energy, the universe and everything in it cannot be infinitely old. The beginning (required by the First Law) could therefore not be very long ago. The message of the Second Law is that the universe is relatively young.

And that brings us to another universal "language" of the universe— the well-established Law of Cause and Effect. Simply stated, it is this: Everything that happens is caused by something else. Every event has a cause that produces an effect. The source (the cause) of the event must have sufficient power and information to produce the specific effect. Even an apparently random event like an explosion (let's say, the Big Bang) has to have the confined energy necessary to produce the explosion and the trigger necessary to start the explosion.

The effect of that supposed Big Bang (the universe) would require that the initial energy confined in the cause must be at least equal to the total energy in the present universe (required by the First Law) and probably somewhat greater than the measureable energy of the universe, given the Second Law's noticeable entropy of the energy used. All that is pure speculation, of course, because no one observed the Big Bang banging. Everything that we can observe and measure about the universe is ordered, structured, and behaves very predictably. Every discipline of science rests on the assurance that everything in the universe is structured, measureable, and predictable!

The Message of the Universe

And that brings us to the constant message that we "hear" from the universe. Everything that we can see and measure and analyze (all true science) shows magnificent design, order, and purpose. The farther we look out into the apparently infinite recesses of space and the deeper our instruments allow us to look into the microscopic structure of molecules, the more complex and awesome becomes our knowledge about the marvelous engineering design in and of everything.

Everything behaves as expected. Whether galaxy, gravity, or ganglion, if we can see it, we can measure it. And every time we measure, it behaves the same. Oh yes, we are finding more about these things all the time and the information is both stunning and wonderful. Everything bears evidence of structure and order—just as we would expect if they were designed! That design is so obvious and so prevalent in everything that many of the recent arguments against design sound rather silly.

Richard Dawkins is perhaps the most well-known and most outspoken anti-theist currently living. He has written a number of bestselling books and has become the darling of the academic world and the often-interviewed spokesman for naturalistic evolution. In his book *The Blind Watchmaker*, he opens with this statement: "Biology is the study of complicated things that give the appearance of having been designed for a purpose."[6] That's quite an admission. In his view, biology (life) looks like it is designed for a purpose, but it's not! Dawkins considers that what we *observe* is design, but what our observations tell us is not true—it is only an *appearance* of design. He thinks this "design" is really evidence of random processes producing what looks like something that has been designed.

It seems as if there is another agenda here. If what the evidence demonstrates (design) is not real, then how can we ever have assurance about anything? Most scientists are honest and straightforward technicians who are driven to understand how things work. Everything our world builds and uses is based on the scientific discovery of principles we can depend on to function in the environments of our lives. If the design that we observe is not really design, how can we trust the buildings that we work in, the bridges that we drive over, or the biological knowledge that our physicians use to keep us well and repair damage?

What About You?

We started this chapter by asking the question "What are you?" Evolutionary theory would tell you that you are nothing more than an accident—"just a bit of slime on a planet" or some sort of galactic "farcical outcome of a chain of accidents."

Science—real, testable, repeatable empirical science—would insist that you are designed. That your biological machinery is not random, that everything in your body is a phenomenal marvel, that the trillions of cells that make up *you* are functioning with a precision that staggers the imagination. Everything in your body has a purpose. Nothing is random. Your DNA is a uniquely designed "program" that caused your body to grow in your mother's womb, guides the development of your specific structure, and keeps your heart pumping—and you alive!

Even when things go wrong and you get sick or have an injury, the design of your body tries to repair itself, fights off invading infections, routes energy to just the right places, and kicks in the necessary processes to help the healing. It takes a *real* accident to undo the design of your body. Yes, the Second Law of Entropy is at work in your body (just like in everything else in the universe), and ultimately all of us will succumb to that law. But in the meantime, we function pretty well.

We are "fearfully and wonderfully made," the Bible tells us (Psalm 139:14). You can be sure of one thing: You are *not* an accident! Everything that can be studied and demonstrated by science verifies that you and I are the product of a magnificent design—and a Designer who personally sculpted the body of the first man and woman and gave them the responsibility of taking care of this planet.

> So God created man in His own image; in the image of God He created him; male and female He created them....And the LORD God formed man of the dust of the ground, and breathed into his nostrils the breath of life; and man became a living soul....And the LORD God said, "It is not good that the man should be alone; I will make him a helper comparable to him."...And the LORD God caused a deep sleep to fall on Adam, and he slept; and He took one of his ribs, and closed up the flesh in its place. Then the rib which the LORD God had taken from man He made into a woman, and He brought her to the man. (Genesis 1:27; 2:7, 18, 21-22)

Pretty awesome! Don't ever think of yourself as an accident.

Notes

1. Atkins, P. *The Daily Telegraph*, April 13, 1996.
2. Stephen Weinberg, cited in Stannard, R. 1993. *Doing Away with God.* Basingstoke, UK: Marshall Pickering, 80.
3. Dawkins, R. 1999. *The Selfish Gene.* New York: Oxford University Press, xi.
4. Hoyle, F. 1994. *The Nature of the Universe.* New York: Penguin Books, 120-121.
5. Newport, F. In U.S. 46% Hold Creationist View of Human Origins. Gallup Politics. Posted on gallup.com June 1, 2012, accessed October 3, 2013.
6. Dawkins, R. 1996. *The Blind Watchmaker.* New York: W. W. Norton & Co., 1.

～ 2 ～
You Are Alive!

This chapter's title may seem obvious to you, but many philosophers and academic theoreticians would suggest that we are not much more than a reactionary batch of chemical elements that function as highly organized biological material (randomly generated, of course). They don't make the TV news or the popular press, since most folks don't like to think about such things, but these theoreticians make a good bit of noise in the academic and theoretical journals.

Actually, their logic is fairly sound—if you believe that everything that now exists is merely the result of simple elements randomly combining over billions of years. After the Big Bang (or whatever started our universe), the energies and early elements formed gases into star clusters, then into galaxies, then....well, you know the basic story. Sometime a few billion years ago (many suggest about 4.5 billion), chemicals in an early "soup" of random material arranged themselves into an organic grouping (maybe something like algae) that could replicate itself. In this scenario, life as we know it has developed over the billions of years since then.

Since that first life was not much more than replicating chemicals, and humans are made of the same basic chemicals, then all living things would be merely self-replicating chemical and protein compositions acting within the basic laws of biology and physics, having been randomly assembled over eons into units that function independently. Whatever value the individual units have is measured only by the degree that they contribute to the evolutionary development of the universe.

Given that sort of thinking, "unfit" units (like unwanted fetuses, deformed children, "useless" old people, or groups that are seen as a drain on a dominant group's development) should be "terminated" to give the rest of the planet more freedom to use its limited resources to survive.

Sounds rather heartless, doesn't it? Actually, according to such thinking, your heart is just a collection of muscles and the foolish idea of a "heartfelt" anything is just nonsense. Your feelings are merely chemical interactions within brain cells that produce electrical impulses reacting to outside stimuli. Your ideas and self-conscious perceptions are just chemical reactions. "You" aren't alive, you are just a collection of chemicals responding to random stimuli.

One contemporary expression of this thinking is reflected in the song "You Are Nothing More Than a Chemical Reaction Inside My Head" by Scottish guitarist Jon Innes on his recent album *That Is the Way of Things*. HBO ran a series for several seasons titled *True Blood*, and one of the most-often cited quotes on Facebook by devotees was "You are nothing more than a lump of muscle with a blood grudge."

Encouraging thoughts, aren't they? No wonder many people feel useless and worthless. Whether or not this sort of reasoning is openly taught in colleges and universities, it dominates the classrooms, TV programs, and songs of our culture, and is both hostile to authority and devoid of any real hope for the future. Life is of small value—except to extend our own apparent existence for some few years, followed by oblivion.

What Is Life Worth?

According to the Motion Picture Association of America, there were over 1.3 billion (yes, *billion*) tickets sold for theater-based films in 2012 in the United States and Canada. More than two-thirds (68 percent) of the entire population went to a movie at least once![1] Nielsen (the company that rates TV shows) records another 140 million viewers watching the top ten TV shows during 2012. The Entertainment Software Association, which tracks sales of video games and hardware, notes that nearly $25 billion-worth of games and hardware was sold in 2011 and that the average American household has at least one game console and its members have been playing those games an average of 12 years.[2]

Lots of people entertain themselves with these powerful visual media.

Here's the problem—the last few decades have seen an alarming increase in violent and horrific films and video games. Of the top 25 movies in 2012 in the U.S. and Canada, all contained violent themes, many of them gratuitous—i.e., the killing was either random or to satisfy personal vengeance or as a solution to personal or governmental problems. Of those movies, there were no G-rated films—only six PG films, 13 PG-13 (six of which were the top-dollar grossing films of 2012), and another six R-rated.[3] Again, all of them contained violent killing. In them, "life" is irrelevant to relationships—murder is an acceptable solution to problems.

And then there are the video games. The Entertainment Software Association notes that only 9 percent of all the video games produced were labeled M (for mature), but those 9 percent accounted for most of the actual sales (in dollars) of all the games. According to the Entertainment Software Rating Board, the M rating stands for:

> MATURE: Content is generally suitable for ages 17 and up. May contain intense violence, blood and gore, sexual content and/or strong language.[4]

Hardly the kind of material one would want most young people filling their minds with, yet a large portion of these "mature" videos are purchased by parents for their children!

What Do TV and Game Violence Do to Children?

No less a prestigious organization than the National Institutes of Health, an arm of the U.S. Department of Health and Human Services, recently funded a study published under the title "The Impact of Electronic Media Violence: Scientific Theory and Research." While the following quote is a bit tough to wade through, it does give a startling and accurate account of how our young people are being exposed to violent behavior.

> Children in the United States spend an average of between 3 and 4 hours per day viewing television. The best studies

15

have shown that more than 60% of programs contain some violence, and about 40% of those contain heavy violence. Children are also spending an increasingly large amount of time playing video games, most of which contain violence. Video game units are now present in 83% of homes with children. In 2004, children spent 49 minutes per day playing video games, and on any given day, 52% of children aged 8-18 years play video games. Video game use peaks during middle childhood, with an average of 65 minutes per day for 8-10-year-olds, and declines to 33 minutes per day for 15-18-year-olds. Most of these games are violent: 94% of games rated (by the video game industry) as appropriate for teens are described as containing violence, and ratings by independent researchers suggest that the real percentage may be even higher. No published study has quantified the violence in games rated 'M' for mature; presumably these are even more likely to be violent.[5]

Ideas Have Consequences

What you believe to be acceptable determines how you think. How you think dictates what you do, and what you do will ultimately dominate your life. Not only do ideas have consequences, but the actions those ideas generate have real and often very demanding consequences.

Our minds are funny things. What we expose ourselves to has an impact on the perspective through which we "filter" the events around us. Sure, we can control a good bit of our ordinary activities, but in a significant emotionally stimulated circumstance, what we have surrounded ourselves with in the past will tend to produce an action (or a reaction) that reflects what we have previously "learned."

Your vocabulary is a good example. Most of us would not use strong, coarse, or filthy language in most social situations. Yet given a sudden pain event, a word (or a string of words) that we have frequently heard or seen used by others (in a movie or TV show or video game) just might "slip" out. Multiply that rather ordinary example by a lifestyle that puts someone in contact with disorderly behavior and the chance of dangerous events increases with the repetitive exposure.

Here's the point—we are surrounded by two major ideas from early childhood through the end of our lives: First, we are nothing more than an accident in an impersonal and random universe; and second, the resulting accidental life is not worth much. You are an expendable assembly of biological material that has no real purpose or meaning. You can be eliminated by others if you get in their way—just as you have the right to terminate others if they interfere with your drive to survive and thrive.

Biblical Contrast

In the first chapter, we spent time demonstrating that everything we know about our existence is purposeful and structured. All empirical evidence shows that everything—including our bodies—is designed and has a reason to exist. Our universe, our solar system, and our planet function and work together to support life like a well-designed piece of machinery. The flaws in the system are either a function of the Second Law (remember entropy) or were messed up by people!

Perhaps a quick trip through how the Bible describes life will help.

To begin with, you are not a plant! That may sound obvious, but according to most scientific philosophy you came from algae (the common ancestor) and have, therefore, just evolved into a more complex reproducing biological unit. The Bible has a very different view.

Things That Move

One quality that sets life apart from plants is movement that is self-directed and independent—any kind of movement that is not connected to the earth or to a food or energy supply. In the Bible, the Hebrew word *ramas* is exclusively applied to animals and to humans, never to plants. The clear meaning and consistent translation of that word depict independent movement—creeping, moving lightly, moving about, walking on all fours, etc.

In spite of fanciful stories, trees do not walk around, flowers do not seasonally migrate, and agricultural crops must be planted and harvested. Living things move around. An animal or person who cannot move or respond is frequently described as being in a "vegetative state." All of us recognize that life moves!

Things That Have Blood

Many centuries ago, God told Moses that the sacrificial system that Israel was to implement must involve the shedding of innocent animal blood because "the life of the flesh is in the blood, and I have given it to you upon the altar to make atonement for your souls; for it is the blood that makes atonement for the soul" (Leviticus 17:11).

Scientists did not discover the elemental principle that "life is in the blood" until well into the 17th century. Now we know—if you lose your blood, you die! By the way, plants don't have blood. They aren't alive. You are!

Things That Have a Soul

In the ancient Hebrew language (the language of the Bible's early books), *nephesh* is the word for "soul." It's used over 680 times in the Bible and used *only* of animal and human life. It's widely used in all kinds of situations related to animal and human circumstances, and seems to stress the emotive side of our lives. Sometimes the word implies a self-awareness, like our personality or passion. Other times the term is just used to recognize life itself.

You and I have a soul. We are alive. Plants and rocks and dirt are not.

Things That Have a Spirit

Once again the Hebrew language supplies a special word for living things—the word *ruwach*. It is most often translated "spirit," but is also translated "wind" and "breath." Apparently, this is the intellectual side of our lives, the self-conscious, thinking side. The same word is used of angelic creatures in Psalm 104:4, where we are told that God "makes His angels spirits." Whatever those heavenly creatures are, they do not have a physical body, but they do "think" and follow orders and bear messages.

You and I have a spirit much like the angels in heaven do. Wow!

Things That Have Life

Life! That word is a term that is never applied to plants in the Bible. Plants are food (Genesis 1:30). The Hebrew word for life is *chay*. Life was *created.* It took the direct intervention of the One who *is* life to create life. The existence of life in any creature is connected inseparably with both soul (*nephesh*) and spirit (*ruwach*).

> In whose hand is the life (*nephesh*) of every living (*chay*) thing, And the breath (*ruwach*) of all mankind? (Job 12:10)

Life is wonderful and marvelous. Life is a quality that God has created that reflects something of who and what He is. Everything we read in the Bible about God's love and intervention for us through Jesus Christ is related to life. Everything else, the universe and the stars, our special planet and all of its functions, is part of the provisions that God has made for life—all life, but especially yours and mine.

To say that you are alive is to summarize all that enables you to be aware of who you are. Being alive gives you the ability to feel—to laugh and to cry. Life brings joy at beautiful things and sorrow at terrible things. Life gives you excitement and boredom, thrills and chills, and temper tantrums and yawns. Life lets you plan for tomorrow, memorize the multiplication tables, hate algebra, love geometry, paint a rose, or design a building. Life gives you the ability to fall in love.

Above all, only life gives life. All the experiments and efforts by the most brilliant scientists using the most sophisticated equipment that money can buy have not been able to produce life from chemicals! Even poor ol' Dolly the cloned sheep started with sheep DNA and required lots of effort and equipment and failures before she was "born." And then the poor dear didn't last long. She was defective in so many ways. Life, real life, takes a male and a female (just like God designed it) to produce another life.

You are alive! You are the product of a mother and a father who themselves were alive. They may or may not have been the ideal parents—but you, YOU are alive. Alive to live and love and thrive and strive and, I sincerely hope, find the One who created life, the One who really does love you and has made provision for you to have *eternal* life! Now that is really living!

Notes
1. Theatrical Market Statistics 2012. Motion Picture Association of America, Inc. Posted on mpaa.org, accessed October 2, 2013.

2. 2012 Sales, Demographics and Usage Data: Essential Facts about the Computer and Video Game Industry. Entertainment Software Association. Posted on theesa.com, accessed October 2, 2013.
3. Theatrical Market Statistics 2012. Motion Picture Association of America, Inc.
4. ESRB Ratings Guide. Entertainment Software Rating Board fact sheet. Posted on esrb.org, accessed September 24, 2013.
5. Huesmann, L. R. 2007. The Impact of Electronic Media Violence: Scientific Theory and Research. *Journal of Adolescent Health*. 41 (Suppl 1): S6-13.

∞ 3 ∞
You Are Not an Animal

I suspect you have heard that humans are the current apex of evolutionary development and, although highly evolved, are really nothing more than advanced mammals. Humans and apes are thought to have split from those early mammals that gave rise to the monkeys of Europe, Asia, and Africa about 20 to 25 million years ago. Humans and great apes—orangutans, gorillas, and chimpanzees—shared a common ancestor that existed around 13 million years ago, and then human ancestors diverged from chimpanzee ancestors around 7 million years ago. *Homo sapiens* (you and I) then mostly likely descended over the last 2 to 3 million years from chimp-like creatures.

At least, that's the party line.

Lots of debate, however, has gone on among the scholars who study fossils. The various "branches" of the human family tree have been sliced and diced every which way, with every new discovery bringing about new ideas about how humans evolved from one branch or another. Some paleoanthropologists (scholars who study human-like fossils) are talking more about a "bush" than a "tree." Since the fossil data are so diverse and partial, there is little agreement among the scholars—other than that *Homo sapiens* did, in fact, come from an ape-like ancestor.

What's the Evidence?

Just what is the hard evidence that you and I evolved from ape-like ancestors? Well, there are a bunch of fossils, that's for sure. Many primate and other fossils are considered to be in the human family tree, most of which are fragmentary and often consist of only partial bones or isolated teeth. More complete skulls and skeletons are very rare. A few, however, are quite interesting.

Lucy is the most famous, discovered by Donald Johanson in 1974 and designated *Australopithecus afarensis*. *Pithecus* is Latin for ape and *austral* means southern, thus her name means "southern ape from Afar," the African region where she was found. She was 3 feet 6 inches tall, estimated to weigh 65 pounds and to be approximately 3.17 million years old. At the time of her discovery, many evolutionists considered *Australopithecus* to be a "long-armed, short-legged knuckle-walker."[1] Most scientists have concluded that Lucy was some form of extinct gibbon. Other *Australopithecus* fossil discoveries and more detailed analyses of Lucy over the next decade pushed Lucy further and further from a direct line of descent to man. However, she is still included in our family tree—because we "know" that humans descended from something like that.

Then along came Ida, discovered by an amateur fossil hunter in Germany in 1983 and named *Darwinius masillae*. Estimated to be some 47 million years old, Ida was a tiny thing, only 19 to 21 inches long, and might have weighed 10 pounds. Ida hit the press as an international "earth-shaking" discovery! She was analyzed by a top-level international team who boldly declared that Ida was the "Rosetta Stone" for understanding early primate evolution.[2] Soon, however, the scientific community admitted that Ida was some kind of lemur and "wasn't even a close relative."[3] In fact, Dr. Erik Seiffert of Stony Brook University in New York said that Ida "is as far removed from the monkey-ape-human ancestry as a primate could be."[4]

Ida was replaced by Ardi (*Ardipithecus ramidus*), another female dated about 4.4 million years old. She stood about 4 feet high and was thought to weigh around 110 pounds. Ardi represented another class of extinct ape fossil; she was found among at least 35 different individuals during 1992 in Ethiopia. One of the more famous scientists who analyzed Ardi was Dr. C. Owen Lovejoy, Kent State University professor of anthropology. Lovejoy insisted that "'Ardi' changes what we know about human evolution."[5] A recent *Science News* article opined that Ardi was "one of the most controversial proposed members of the human evolutionary family, considered an ancient ape by some skeptical scientists....a mix of monkey, ape and hominid characteristics."[6]

If you have been paying attention, you will have noted that all of these famous fossils are rather short and small and have all the characteristics of primates. That is, they are mid-size apes with only a few features not seen in modern chimpanzees, gibbons, lemurs, bonobos, or orangutans. The best that can be said of them is that they are unusual and extinct apes. They are not human—not even close. Yet the story of human evolution is told so often that everyone just seems to believe it to be true.

What Difference Does It Make?

The acceptance of the evolutionary story has influenced just about every form of sociological thinking. This is particularly true among the various disciplines that impact how we think about ourselves and our "fellow animals," the "non-humans." I hope that sounds a bit foolish to you, but it is absolutely no joke. As far as the overwhelming part of the academic, legal, political, philosophical, and scientific world is concerned, you *are* an animal and you share this planet with "fellow life forms" that deserve—in some cases—better treatment than humans.

Australian philosopher Dr. Peter Singer is currently Professor of Bioethics at Princeton University and a Laureate Professor at the Centre for Applied Philosophy and Public Ethics at the University of Melbourne. He is most well-known for his 1975 book *Animal Liberation*, frequently referred to as a "canonical text" on animal rights and animal liberation theory. That book and subsequent publications have formed something of the core beliefs of the People for the Ethical Treatment of Animals (PETA).

In Dr. Singer's article "All Animals Are Equal," he writes, "I am urging that we extend to other species the basic principle of equality that most of us recognize should be extended to all members of our own species."[7] That platform has become the basic philosophical justification for many strange bedfellows.

PETA founder Ingrid Newkirk flaunts the position that animals are other nations, not slaves, hamburgers, handbags, cheap toys, and test tubes with whiskers. Today, Newkirk insists that "although our newspapers are full of stories of sophisticated communication in the animal world, and no one doubts that the other animals—we being just one—experience maternal love, pain, joy, loneliness, and fear, we dismiss those feelings as inconsequential....A full-grown horse or dog is beyond comparison a more rational as well as a more conversable animal, than an infant of a day or a week or even a month old."[8] She and Peter Singer agree: Killing a human infant or deformed human child—or even a "useless" elderly person—is no different from putting an animal to sleep.

Those earlier 1980s and 1990s efforts gave birth to the Nonhuman Rights Project, formed in 2007 after a decade of ceaseless lecturing and posturing by the various anti-religious and pro-animal rights movements. According to Steven M. Wise, President of the Nonhuman Rights Project, Inc., its mission is:

> Through education and litigation, to change the common law status of at least some nonhuman animals from mere "things," which lack the capacity to possess any legal right, to "persons," who possess such fundamental rights as bodily integrity and bodily liberty, and those other legal rights to which evolving standards of morality, scientific discovery, and human experience entitle them....[Dr. Wise] teaches "Animal Rights Jurisprudence" at several law schools and is the author of...*Rattling the Cage—Toward Legal Rights for Animals*; [and] *Drawing the Line—Science and the Case for Animal Rights*.[9]

All of the above is to make you aware of two things: One, the majority of modern science is convinced that you are an animal—highly evolved, but an animal nonetheless. And two, the social movements among activist political and legal circles are inexorably moving toward legalizing "animal rights"—to the detriment and potential exclusion of human uniqueness and value.

You, as far as the majority of world thinkers go, are an animal.

What About Empirical Science?

In spite of the academic shouting, posturing, and foot stomping, there is a good bit of hard scientific evidence that you are *not* an animal—especially not anything like a chimpanzee. Let's explore the basics.

Common Design

As discussed in the first chapter, the observational evidence is overwhelming—everything we can observe and test has clear evidence of design and purpose. Since that is so clearly expressed, we would expect that land animals (especially mammals) would share some common designs. For instance, the internal skeletons of land animals are strong and sturdy, designed to carry weight and allow for repetitive motion. It should be no surprise, then, that primates and humans have similar skeletal features. Nor should it be a surprise that land animals (especially those who share similar lifestyles) would have internal and external characteristics that are pretty much the same. Muscular structures and internal organs would be similar since all of these creatures have active lives, eat, sleep, and reproduce with basic functions that require common designs.

It should be no surprise to scientists, then, to find a commonality in the design programming—the DNA. Similarities between chimpanzees and humans would be expected (both have many similar characteristics), but drawing the inference that humans have therefore descended from chimp-like ancestors is a stretch.

In fact, several studies have shown that humans have genetic data that are very similar to mice and kangaroos. Not much appears in the popular press about our relationship to either group, however, since that doesn't fit the majority opinions of the academics. More interesting yet is that some researchers have found that we share half our genes (DNA) with bananas. Well, since both chimps and humans eat bananas, why not? As long as the comparison is based on selected "lettering" of the DNA strands, just about any conclusion is possible.

Empirical DNA Research

It is rather common today to compare DNA similarities among humans to determine relationships. The more similar the patterns are, the more closely related the people are said to be. We often hear such stories from various court cases or paternity searches. That really works well—from human to human! But when one tries to apply the same logic from human to chimp—or from human to kangaroo or mice or bananas—the testing logic breaks down.

To begin with, the testable data (lab work) must be interpreted. While we can be relatively sure that calculations of the genetic similarities between certain creatures are accurate, the relationship between those creatures depends on the assumptions that are made about them. With human beings, we have many written records (archives, birth records, etc.) that help us establish the "family tree." Those historical accounts give more certainty to the conclusions of the test data.

Once we get beyond known records, however, we are inferring and assuming relationships based on the extrapolation of our known data. With humans, we can be fairly sure. With ancestry beyond written records, we must base the conclusions on interpretative inference. In science, the difference is called *operational science* versus *historical science*. Operational science refers to testing performed according to the scientific method (observing, testing, reproducing the same test and getting the same results). Historical science is a form of forensic study—that is, using either eyewitness accounts (if available) or clues that must be interpreted.

Since no one observes a chimp producing a human today, the scientific method is not possible. What can be (and is) done is comparing the DNA information of humans with chimpanzees and interpreting the results based on the clues of similar anatomy and design. Much of the work done over the past decade has concentrated on specific areas of the DNA chemicals that impact observable changes. Within the past few years, many studies have concentrated on blood chemistry and brain cells—assuming (correctly) that blood and the brain perform pretty important functions! Differences, therefore, might provide clues to the relationship between various creatures.

Dr. Jeffrey Tomkins ran one of the largest gene sequencing labs in the country at Clemson University. He now heads ICR's research on human-chimp similarities. Many scientific research programs are funded by government programs, and their results are therefore available to all scientists. Dr. Tomkins has taken their data and has found some startling admissions by the researchers. Instead of the fabled 98 percent similarity touted in the popular literature for several years, researchers are now admitting that the differences are much wider—as much as 30 percent wider! And those differences are among the key chemistries of blood and the brain.

I won't attempt to list all of the technical data. (You can find this on the ICR website if you are interested.) Suffice it to say, dramatic differences exist! The research has been tissue-specific (same types of cells and locations). For instance, white blood cells from living humans, chimps, and orangutans were compared because they are the most similar type of cell known between humans and apes. The scientists were surprised to find that in over 1,500 different regions major differences were obvious between the human and chimp cells.[10]

In 2012, a study was performed on the genetic chemistry in human and chimp brain cells that impacts neurological disorders and cancers. Overall, 1,055 genes demonstrated significantly different patterns—468 of which were "highly diverse." These are the genes that control other genes and determine when and if proteins in the cell are modified. These genes showed marked differences and were key to controlling regions in the genome for brain cell activity.[11]

Well, what does all of this serious study mean? Simply this. There are profound genetic differences between humans and apes—such profound differences that there is no logical evolutionary connection between the two types of creatures. These cutting-edge studies fit closely with the biblical message that you are not a "monkey's uncle."

All kidding aside, we may chuckle at the antics of chimps and orangutans we see in a zoo, but most of us are aware that these creatures are far removed from us—if by no other observation than by the simple behavioral and anatomical distinctions. Popular "scientific" shows like *Nova* and *Discover* may present stunning photography of animal behavior in the wild with professional voice-overs that ascribe human behavior and thought to those animals, but empirical, testable, repeatable science does not bear out those "documentaries."

Science demonstrates a vast difference. Science insists that humans are not chimpanzees. Science confirms what the Bible teaches. You and I are created in the image of God and bear the responsibility to care for the planet and the animals that share its resources with us.

Notes

1. 1971. Australopithecus, a Long-Armed Short-Legged, Knuckle-Walker. *Science News.* 100 (22): 357.
2. Common Ancestor Of Humans, Modern Primates? 'Extraordinary' Fossil Is 47 Million Years Old. *ScienceDaily.* Posted on sciencedaily.com May 19, 2009, accessed September 25, 2013.
3. Controversial "Ida" Fossil No Missing Link. *CBS News.* Posted on cbsnews.com October 22, 2009, accessed September 25, 2013.
4. Fossil Skeleton Known as Ida Is No Ancestor of Humans. The Associated Press, October 22, 2009.
5. Professor: Man Did Not Evolve From Chimpanzee-like Apes. Kent State University news release, October 1, 2009.
6. Bower, B. 2013. Ardi's kind had a skull fit for a hominid. *Science News.* 183 (10): 13.
7. Singer, P. 1989. All Animals Are Equal. In *Animal Rights and Human Obligations.* Regan, T. and P. Singer, eds. New Jersey: Prentice-Hall, 148-162.
8. Are Animal and Human Life Equal? *ABC News.* Posted on abcnews.go.com August 31, 2001, accessed October 2, 2013.
9. About Us. Nonhuman Rights Project fact sheet. Posted on nonhumanrightsproject.org, accessed October 3, 2013.
10. Tomkins, J. 2013. Epigenetics Proves Humans and Chimps Are Different. *Acts & Facts.* 42 (1): 11-12.
11. Ibid.

∾ 4 ∾

You Are Unique

There is a passage in C. S. Lewis' second Narnian chronicle, *Prince Caspian*, where Aslan (the lion who represents the Lord Jesus in the allegory) tells young Caspian:

> "You come of the Lord Adam and the Lady Eve....And that is both honor enough to erect the head of the poorest beggar, and shame enough to bow the shoulders of the greatest emperor on earth. Be content."[1]

Good counsel. We all go through various episodes where we feel like we are not worth much—and conversely have occasions where we are sure that we are superior to the rest of the world. Neither evaluation is right. No one is insignificant and no one is irreplaceable. You are, indeed, unique! No one else is just like you, and no one else can *be* you. Be content!

Recombination

You probably remember that humans have 23 pairs of chromosomes, for a total of 46. Twenty-two of those look pretty much the same in all humans, but in women the smallest pair consists of two X chromosomes, while in men the pair consists of one X and one Y chromosome. Those are the genetic instructions that make the biggest difference!

Within those 46 chromosomes are some 20 to 30 thousand genes, each "written" with the four DNA base pairs A, T, G, and C (the nucleotides adenine, cytosine, guanine, and thymine) in the human genome. Nobody is really sure how many genes the human genome has because the 3 billion-plus "instructions" are responsible for growing you during nine months in the womb and then for keeping the 3 trillion or so cells of your body working and percolating over your lifetime!

By the way, grape plants have about 30,000 genes and chickens have around 17,000. The *number* of genes isn't important. It's what the genes and their genetic regulators "say" that's important. And it's that which makes you unique!

When you were conceived, one half of the genetic "instructions" from your mom and one half from your dad came together in an absolutely unique combination. The math on this is incredible. No one has been able to calculate the odds of what transpires at conception, but it is surely accurate to say that there is no human being in all of history or the future who will have precisely the same information in their genome as you (or me). This is even true for identical twins, where one fertilized egg (zygote) splits and forms two embryos. Even though they share the same initial "information," when the zygote splits, modifications to the use of the DNA sequence make even identical twins unique individuals.

Becoming You

Dr. Randy Guliuzza is an engineer and a medical doctor with a Masters in Public Health from Harvard University. He joined ICR as a national lecturer after retiring a Lt. Colonel from the U.S. Air Force, where he served as Flight Surgeon and Chief of Aerospace Medicine. One of Dr. Guliuzza's specialties, as you might imagine, is the stunning wonder and design of the human body. His writings and lectures on the development of a new person in the womb are especially enlightening.

Here is some of what Dr. Guliuzza writes about the way you and I began.

The real star of the show, however, is the developing baby, who was once viewed as a passive object being built by the mother's body. Nothing could be further from the truth. In terms of guiding implantation into the uterus all the way to breastfeeding, it is the baby/placenta unit that is the dynamic force in the orchestration of its own destiny.

The baby is a completely new individual, with unique genetic material that expresses foreign markers on his cells that are not recognized as "self" by the mother. The mother's immune system should destroy the new baby's first cells within just a few cell divisions, but substances secreted by the placenta and baby promote a complex suppression of the maternal immune response only within the implantation site of the uterus....

The mother's body is now under the control of a new person...hormones produced by the baby induce adaptations in the mother's body that are absolutely necessary for the baby's survival....So it is the mother who is essentially passive, responding to signals emanating from the baby—even at times to her own detriment. Scientific research has shown that while the woman's reproductive organs and body are indispensable, they are not enough; it takes a baby to make a baby.[2]

There's a lot more to "you" that Dr. Guliuzza describes in his book *Made in His Image*.[3] If you would like to gain an appreciation of how "fearfully and wonderfully made" you are (Psalm 139:14), you might want to get a copy of that book. You really are unique!

The Image of God

As wonderful as the physical human body is, the really unique part is that we were designed by the Creator to bear His image.

Then God said, "Let Us make man in Our image, according to Our likeness; let them have dominion over the fish of the sea, over the birds of the air, and over the cattle, over all the earth and over every creeping thing that creeps on the earth." So God created man in His own image; in the image of God He created him; male and female He created them. (Genesis 1:26-27)

Theologians and students of Scripture have been pondering this passage since it was recorded. Just what is it that God created in His own image? What is God's image? All human beings have something special in their design that makes them different from every other living thing on the planet. That image includes both the physical shape and the intrinsic intelligence and spiritual capabilities that separate us from the animals.

Only One of Each

When the Creator made man on Day Six, He made only one male and one female body. All other life forms in the air, in the water, and on and under the earth were made at least in the hundreds of pairs, if not thousands or millions. They were "abundant" and "filled" the air and sea and land.

Not so with Adam and Eve.

> And the LORD God formed man of the dust of the ground, and breathed into his nostrils the breath of life; and man became a living being....And the LORD God caused a deep sleep to fall on Adam, and he slept; and He took one of his ribs, and closed up the flesh in its place. Then the rib which the LORD God had taken from man He made into a woman, and He brought her to the man. (Genesis 2:7, 21-22)

It is worth noting that a very precise term, the Hebrew word *yatsar*, is used about the "forming" of Adam and the "making" of Eve. *Yatsar* is a "hands on" verb used to describe personal involvement like an artist painting a picture or a sculptor shaping a figure. The same word is used in Psalm 94:9: "He who *formed* the eye, shall He not see?"

Adam was the first man (1 Corinthians 15:47) and was unique from everything else that had been made.

Next, the Creator took some "rib" from Adam and "made" a woman. The English translations don't quite do justice to what happened. *Tesla* is the Hebrew word translated "rib." Every other time it appears in the Bible it is translated "side." Surely what God took from Adam would have included a rib, but there was muscle and other tissue as well, which is why Adam later said, "This is now bone of my bones And flesh of my flesh; She shall be called Woman, Because she was taken out of Man" (Genesis 2:23).

In both cases—with the handful of dirt and the piece of Adam's side—God *formed* and *made* the independent and unique bodies of Adam and Eve.

Our Body Can Be a Temple for God's Spirit

You may be familiar with the biblical teaching that our physical body becomes a "temple" for the presence of the Spirit of God after we have been twice-born. This is an amazing thing! After our conversion and the spiritual "birth" that God causes to happen (more on this in the next chapter), our unique and spectacular bodies are suitable "hosts" for the Third Person of the Creator God (1 Corinthians 3:16).

This is mysterious, to be sure, but there are a number of biblical reasons why this is important for us to catch because we have been designed to share the image of God. Obviously, the God of the Bible is not confined to the shape of a human being (John 4:24), but we are specifically told that Jesus *became* man and took on our nature (Philippians 2:5-8).

Stick with me here. One of the reasons we are unique from animals is that we share the same kind of body that God had in mind for His Son—even before the world was ever created. Check out these Bible references.

- Jesus Christ is the visible form of God.

  And the Word became flesh and dwelt among us, and we beheld His glory, the glory as of the only begotten of the Father, full of grace and truth. (John 1:14)

  Jesus said to him, "…He who has seen Me has seen the Father." (John 14:9)

  For in Him dwells all the fullness of the Godhead bodily. (Colossians 2:9)

- God has always appeared on Earth to us in human form.

  Abraham: Three men were standing by him….And the LORD said, "Shall I hide from Abraham what I am doing?"… So the LORD went His way as soon as He had finished speaking with Abraham; and Abraham returned to his place. Now the two angels came to Sodom in the evening. (Genesis 18:2, 17, 33–19:1)

Jacob: Then Jacob was left alone; and a Man wrestled with him until the breaking of day....So Jacob called the name of the place Peniel: "For I have seen God face to face, and my life is preserved." (Genesis 32:24, 30)

Daniel: "I was watching in the night visions, And behold, One like the Son of Man, Coming with the clouds of heaven!" (Daniel 7:13)

Peter, James, John: Jesus...led them up on a high mountain by themselves; and He was transfigured before them. His face shone like the sun, and His clothes became as white as the light. (Matthew 17:1-2)

- Jesus Christ was designed before the foundation of the world.

"A body You have prepared for Me." (Hebrews 10:5)

...the Lamb slain from the foundation of the world. (Revelation 13:8)

He indeed was foreordained before the foundation of the world, but was manifest in these last times for you. (1 Peter 1:20)

Our Earthly Bodies Are Not Perfect Now

Beloved, now we are children of God; and it has not yet been revealed what we shall be, but we know that when He is revealed, we shall be like Him, for we shall see Him as He is. (1 John 3:2)

Something that Adam and Eve possessed at creation, before their rebellion, is restored at the moment of the "second" birth. That something was at least part of the image of God. It may well have been the eternal and spiritual part of humanity that we *do not* possess prior to salvation. What we possess now will, however, be changed before we can be "as He is" during eternity. The face-to-face fellowship with God that Adam and Eve knew prior to their rebellion (Genesis 1:29; 2:8, 16; 3:8-10) was taken away, and the relationship between the Creator and His crowning creation still needs to be resolved.

We Will Be Eternally Human

One of the greatest promises that God has given to us is that when everything has been wrapped up and God restores the universe to what we loosely call "heaven," we will be made like Him! Vast changes will be made to our bodies when we join the Lord Jesus after the resurrection, but we will still have human form.

> So also is the resurrection of the dead. The body is sown in corruption, it is raised in incorruption. It is sown in dishonor, it is raised in glory. It is sown in weakness, it is raised in power. It is sown a natural body, it is raised a spiritual body. (1 Corinthians 15:42-44)

> Behold, I tell you a mystery: We shall not all sleep, but we shall all be changed—in a moment, in the twinkling of an eye, at the last trumpet. For the trumpet will sound, and the dead will be raised incorruptible, and we shall be changed. For this corruptible must put on incorruption, and this mortal must put on immortality. (1 Corinthians 15:51-53)

Obviously, these contrasts between the earthly and the heavenly reflect the awful judgment of Genesis 3, when everything in the whole creation began to fall apart (Romans 8:22). We'll cover more of this in the next chapter, but what is of consequence here as far as the image of God in man is concerned is the clear acknowledgement in Scripture that our earthly bodies, while created eternal and perfect, do not now fit the requirements for the "new heaven and the new earth" that will come (2 Peter 3:13).

Three Important Points

All these Scriptures reveal three very important points about the image of God that was created in both male and female on Day Six of the creation week.

1) There was an eternal part to us that no longer exists—until we are given eternal life at the point of salvation. Apparently, Adam

and Eve possessed that quality when they were created.

2) The human body form is directly connected throughout Scripture with the body of our Lord Jesus—both in His appearances prior to His entry into this world and after His resurrection.

3) The mortal body that humanity is now born into after the terrible judgment pronounced by God in Genesis 3 must be changed into a suitable immortal body that will be compatible with the eternal body of the Lord Jesus.

Whatever God did for Adam and Eve that made them in His image He did not do for the rest of creation. As marvelous as their many life forms and functions are, none of the sea, air, or land creatures can fellowship with the Creator—except man. Yes, one day every tongue in the universe will confess the Lordship of Jesus Christ in an open assembly around the Throne in heaven (Romans 14:11). Now, however, mankind alone is afforded the opportunity to be redeemed and reconciled to the great Creator.

The image of God in humans became "dead in trespasses and sins" (Ephesians 2:1) because of the horrible rebellion of Adam, but we are now given the opportunity to receive the "guarantee of our inheritance until the redemption of the purchased possession" (Ephesians 1:14). We humans—and humans alone—can be born "again to a living hope through the resurrection of Jesus Christ from the dead, to an inheritance incorruptible and undefiled and that does not fade away, reserved in heaven for you, who are kept by the power of God through faith for salvation ready to be revealed in the last time" (1 Peter 1:3-5).

Notes
1. Lewis, C. S. 1994. *Prince Caspian*. New York: HarperCollins, 233.
2. Guliuzza, R. J. 2009. Made in His Image: Human Gestation. *Acts & Facts*. 38 (2): 10.
3. Guliuzza, R. J. 2009. *Made in His Image: Examining the complexities of the human body*. Dallas, TX: Institute for Creation Research.

∽ 5 ∽

You Can Be Twice-Born

You may think this chapter title is some sort of special appeal—but it is really a unique privilege only available to humans. I hope you have been convinced that you are not the result of random particles bouncing around for billions of years and that your life is really something special—a creation of the life-giving God of eternity. Furthermore, I trust that you have a bit more appreciation of yourself, since you are unique in the entire universe and your life is much more than a more-complex chimpanzee!

Now comes the best part!

The One who created you and formed you with His image has made it entirely possible for you to be "re"-created—yep, created a second time with the eternal part that was lost by our first parents, Adam and Eve. Jesus called the process being "born again" (John 3:3). That term has been bandied about so much that it might take a bit of clarification, so let's tackle the subject using just the information from the Bible.

The Beginning

You may remember that when God created humans He made only one of each—one man and one woman. Designed into each of them was everything that could be included in God's image—except the "omni" parts (omnipotent, omniscient, omnipresent). Everything else was there. They had the unique shape that God had in mind for Jesus before the world was ever created. They had the eternal spirit and the magnificent intelligence that enabled them to worship their Creator, fellowship with Him, and rule the planet for Him. They were as good as God could make them (everything worked flawlessly, by the way). They were complete in every way and had the entire "very good" planet at their disposal.

> Then God saw everything that He had made, and indeed it was very good. So the evening and the morning were the sixth day. (Genesis 1:31)

God even made a special garden for them. Don't think of a corn and potato patch, think of an estate—like a magnificent castle and sculptured grounds (well, maybe not a castle).

> Then God blessed them, and God said to them, "Be fruitful and multiply; fill the earth and subdue it; have dominion over the fish of the sea, over the birds of the air, and over every living thing that moves on the earth." (Genesis 1:28)

> The Lord God planted a garden eastward in Eden....Then the Lord God took the man and put him in the garden of Eden to tend and keep it. (Genesis 2:8, 15)

They were put there with all the freedom that could possibly be given to people, with the instructions to "tend and keep it" and "have dominion over" all of the animal life on the planet and to "subdue" the earth (that is, to understand and use the all resources God had created and made). Wow! What a job description. That makes a CEO look like a stock boy.

All they had to do was listen to the few instructions they were given and rule the planet! Don't forget, God had designed into their DNA all the information that would ever be used for every human who would later come into existence! Their genes would have been perfect—no mutations, no "misspellings," no misfiring instructions. Perfect! (Just in case you haven't figured it out yet, you and I are *not* perfect.) Not only were they physically magnificent, but they were intellectually, emotionally, and spiritually complete as well.

Whatever you and I "are" we have inherited from Adam and Eve. All of the personality traits were part of their DNA. All of the planet's varied population groups and characteristics come from those two. All of the widely distributed intelligence and aptitude distinctions were present in the capacities inherent in those first parents. Can you imagine what it might have been like if Adam and Eve hadn't messed things up at the beginning?

The Problem

That is exactly what happened. In spite of their complete abilities and opportunities, Adam and Eve gave in to the *possibility* of "one-up-manship." They listened to a seductive argument that *seemed* to give them the chance to be equal with God (or at least gain enough smarts to get out from under His authority). The result of their decision was disaster—for everything and everyone!

Although the record in Genesis is written as actual history, we have a tough time relating to the specific circumstances. To begin with, we are not perfect and our planet is full of disasters. That makes it difficult to understand what took place—especially with the serpent and two rather unusual trees.

> And out of the ground the LORD God made every tree grow that is pleasant to the sight and good for food. The tree of life was also in the midst of the garden, and the tree of the knowledge of good and evil....And the LORD God commanded the man, saying, "Of every tree of the garden you may freely eat; but of the tree of the knowledge of good and evil you shall not eat, for in the day that you eat of it you shall surely die." (Genesis 2:9, 16-17)

It's not really clear just what these two special trees were. Obviously, they were "good for food"—that was one of the reasons that Eve was snookered into eating the fruit of the forbidden tree. But just what type of fruit-food was produced is not said. We are later told in the book of Revelation that the tree of life will be replanted in the new earth, that many of those trees will line the great river that will come out of the capital city, New Jerusalem, and that "the leaves of the tree were for the healing of the nations" (Revelation 22:2). Whatever that tree was, it was designed by God to have life-giving properties!

But the other tree—the tree of the knowledge of good and evil—just what was *that* tree? Apparently, it was good as food. Eve thought so. God said so. So what was evil about it? Well, two things. First, God had set a prohibition on it. Just the one tree. All others were OK. Remember, God is the Creator. He is the Boss! He has the right (with His own stuff—the creation) to make whatever restrictions He wants.

> But indeed, O man, who are you to reply against God? Will the thing formed say to him who formed it, "Why have you made me like this?" Does not the potter have power over the clay, from the same lump to make one vessel for honor and another for dishonor? (Romans 9:20-21)

That should have been enough. Adam and Eve had total freedom and unlimited authority to subdue and have dominion over the planet. They had only *one* restriction—one limited sphere of responsibility—don't eat the food of *that* tree! The warning was simple: Eat that fruit and you will *know* evil—and you will die. They were immortal. They were perfect and complete. They had the whole planet before them. They had everything! Except that one itty bitty tree.

The Result

Well, you know what happened. First Eve and then Adam disobeyed the one restriction God had set for them, and the warning became reality. They ate and they died—spiritually that instant and physically over time. They were made out of dirt, God reminded them, and they would return to dirt. You and I (descended from their DNA) have, as a result, been born "dead" spiritually and must be "made alive" by the only One who has the power to do that—the Creator.

We could spend a lot of time on the serpent and his role, but the key parts are enough for our discussion. The Bible implies that Satan himself was involved in this event, either by controlling what the serpent said or by taking that shape to talk with Eve (Revelation 12:9). Either way, Eve was manipulated into disobedience by a three-stage temptation:

1) Did God really say that? (Genesis 3:1)
   – Doubt about the truth of the Word of God.

2) God lied to you! (Genesis 3:4)
   – Denial of the ability of God to do what He says.

3) God is withholding secrets from you. (Genesis 3:5)
   – Denigration of the character of God.

Adam, however, was not fooled (1 Timothy 2:14)! He was right there, listening to the conversation—and never said a word of warning or caution. He just let it happen. And then He willingly, consciously, knowingly, flagrantly disobeyed!

Nothing has changed in all the millennia since. Our temptations still come in that same sequence and with the same results. We sin, and the wages of sin is death (Romans 6:23)! There are no exclusions, no exceptions, "for all have sinned and fall short of the glory of God" (Romans 3:23). Because of Adam and Eve's sin, we are "dead in trespasses and sins" and are "by nature children of wrath" (Ephesians 2:1, 3).

The Rescue

Well, we're stuck! Unless the Creator who made us in His image "so loved the world that He gave His only begotten Son, that whoever believes in Him should not perish but have everlasting life" (John 3:16). And, of course, that is exactly what happened! God's Word gives us the basics of what God did for us.

First, God came into our world and became just like us: Jesus was the name He took.

Christ Jesus, who, being in the form of God, did not consider it robbery to be equal with God, but made Himself of no reputation, taking the form of a bondservant, and coming in the likeness of men. (Philippians 2:5-7)

And the Word became flesh and dwelt among us, and we beheld His glory, the glory as of the only begotten of the Father, full of grace and truth. (John 1:14)

Therefore, in all things He had to be made like His brethren, that He might be a merciful and faithful High Priest in things pertaining to God, to make propitiation for the sins of the people. (Hebrews 2:17)

Even though we were full of sin and "dead" because of those sins, Jesus gave His sinless life in our place and paid the "wages" of our death so we could live.

For we do not have a High Priest who cannot sympathize with our weaknesses, but was in all points tempted as we are, yet without sin. (Hebrews 4:15)

Surely He has borne our griefs And carried our sorrows; Yet we esteemed Him stricken, Smitten by God, and afflicted. But He was wounded for our transgressions, He was bruised for our iniquities; The chastisement for our peace was upon Him, And by His stripes we are healed. (Isaiah 53:4-5)

For Christ also suffered once for sins, the just for the unjust, that He might bring us to God, being put to death in the flesh but made alive by the Spirit. (1 Peter 3:18)

The substitution of the sinless life of God's Son, Jesus Christ, was both legally satisfactory and infinitely sufficient to make possible our "new creation" as spiritually alive children adopted into God's eternal family.

But God, who is rich in mercy, because of His great love with which He loved us, even when we were dead in trespasses, made us alive together with Christ (by grace you have been saved), and raised us up together, and made us sit together in the heavenly places in Christ Jesus, that in the ages to come He might show the exceeding riches of His grace in His kindness toward us in Christ Jesus. (Ephesians 2:4-7)

For by grace you have been saved through faith, and that not of yourselves; it is the gift of God, not of works, lest anyone should boast. For we are His workmanship, created in Christ Jesus for good works, which God prepared beforehand that we should walk in them. (Ephesians 2:4-10)

That you put on the new man which was created according

to God, in true righteousness and holiness. (Ephesians 4:24)

The new creation that God implements for those who become His eternally adopted children is completed when any human being acts on the information God reveals to us and believes that God is telling the whole truth.

> For God so loved the world that He gave His only begotten Son, that whoever believes in Him should not perish but have everlasting life. For God did not send His Son into the world to condemn the world, but that the world through Him might be saved. (John 3:16-17)

> In this the love of God was manifested toward us, that God has sent His only begotten Son into the world, that we might live through Him. (1 John 4:9)

> If you confess with your mouth the Lord Jesus and believe in your heart that God has raised Him from the dead, you will be saved. For with the heart one believes unto righteousness, and with the mouth confession is made unto salvation. (Romans 10:9-10)

Actually, it's pretty simple, isn't it? Adam and Eve refused to believe that God was telling them the truth and died because of their foolishness. God still loved them and all of the people that would come into the world through them, so He provided the *only* solution possible: He gave Himself to solve the problem. He came into the world as the Lord Jesus, took our form and nature, lived a human life, was subjected to every kind of temptation and problem that humans could ever face and did not blow it like Adam did. He willingly accepted unjust condemnation and death—for our sakes—and then, to prove that He was really God in the flesh, came back again from death (after paying our "wages") as the resurrected Lord.

Now He sits in heaven as the Advocate (defending lawyer) on our behalf, acting as the eternal High Priest interceding for us, all the time preparing a place for us to live with Him forever. And one day He—that same Jesus who died for us and rose again from the grave—will come to Earth again as King of kings and Lord of lords to end the rule of the

Enemy and make a "new heavens and a new earth in which righteousness dwells" (2 Peter 3:13)!

Recapitulation

Someone has said that you shouldn't repeat things, just recapitulate. So here goes.

First—you are not an accident! You are a wonderfully designed and magnificent human being with the responsibility and intelligence to care for this planet.

Second—you are alive! You are not an impersonal collection of molecules with mere chemical reactions for brains. You have blood in your veins! You move, you emote, you think, you love and hate and do math and make music and make mistakes. You are alive!!

Third—you are not an animal! No matter how much chimps and bonobos and orangutans look like Uncle Harry, they are *not* Uncle Harry! Everybody knows that. There is so much difference between human beings and animals. Gracious! The difference is profound—and scientific studies are proving that more and more each day. Don't ever think of yourself as an animal. Don't act like one. Don't dress like one. Don't smell like one. You bear the image of the Creator God!

Fourth—you are unique! There is nobody else in the entire universe like you! Not in the past and not ever in the future. God has placed you here for a specific purpose and no one else in the world can do what you do. Find out what that is. Learn what only you can do. Get rid of all that evolutionary baggage. You are God's creation! Your origins matter!!!

Finally—because you are not an accident of random atoms, because you are an alive human being, created in God's own image, unique in all the universe—God loves you! God loves you with an eternal love that will never go away. No matter what you have done or think you are, God has made it possible for you to become His child! You can be twice-born!

Jesus had two important things to say about all this that I will leave you with. One is an invitation. The other is a promise.

"Come to Me, all you who labor and are heavy laden, and

I will give you rest. Take My yoke upon you and learn from Me, for I am gentle and lowly in heart, and you will find rest for your souls. For My yoke is easy and My burden is light." (Matthew 11:28-30)

"And this is the will of Him who sent Me, that everyone who sees the Son and believes in Him may have everlasting life; and I will raise him up at the last day." (John 6:40)

When people hear the earth is billions of years old... what do you say?

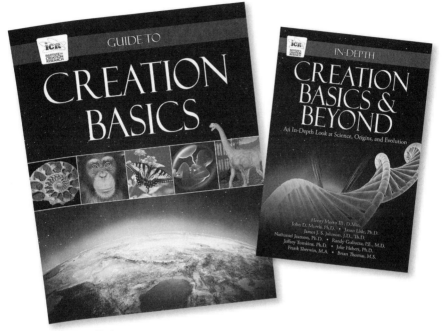

How well do you know the fundamentals of creation? The hard-cover *Guide to Creation Basics*—authored by ICR scientists and scholars—is filled with full-color illustrations and loaded with information from science, history, and the Bible that shows God's ingenuity, power, and care in creating our world.

Creation Basics & Beyond: An In-Depth Look at Science, Origins, and Evolution offers a thorough, yet understandable, overview of the essential questions involved in the creation-evolution debate. Written and reviewed by experts and organized into short, readable chapters, this book shows how the scientific evidence does not support evolution but strongly confirms the biblical account of creation.

To order, call **800.628.7640** or **visit www.icr.org/store**. Also available through Kindle, NOOK, and iBookstore.